CW00401931

Top Air Fryer Cookbook

Fabulous Air Fryer Recipes To Improve Your Diet And Make Cooking Fun Again

Mary Stourbrook

Copyright © [2022] [Mary Stourbrook]

All rights reserved

All rights for this book here presented belong exclusively to the author. Usage or reproduction of the text is forbidden and requires a clear consent of the author in case of expectations.

ISBN - 9798834897286

Table of Contents

EXCLUSIVE BONUS

40 Weight Loss Recipes

&

14 Days Meal Plan

Scan the QR-Code and receive
the FREE download:

What is an Air Fryer?

An air fryer is similar to a standard kitchen oven. They cook your food in a similar fashion and you can make a lot of the same dishes in either.

You can bake, roast, and grill a range of dishes using your air fryer. The machine contains heating elements that get hot and cook the food through radiation and convection. Air fryers also contain a fan that encourages more of the hot air to flow around the inner compartment of the machine. This speeds up the cooking process and results in crispy, delicious foods.

The air fryer has been around for years and it was originally created and patented by Philips Electronic Company. The patent covers a kitchen appliance that can be used to create healthy alternatives to a deep fryer by using little or no oil and hot air.

Based on this, it's clear to see why people love the air fryer. Most people buy this type of kitchen gadget to create healthier meals and ditch the deep fryer.

Since the air fryer requires very little or no oil at all to cook the ingredients, you can reduce the calories and saturated fat content in your dishes. Even for those who aren't on a health kick, the air fryer has its advantages and we will discuss these a little later in the book.

How Do Air Fryers Work?

Air fryers cook your ingredients using several heating elements that are inserted into the top of the machine. The inside of the air fryer contains a mesh basket.

When you place your food in the mesh basket and shut the life of the air fryer, the heating elements begin to cook the food. A fan inside the machine helps to push hot air around the inner compartment to help the food cook quicker and more evenly.

Unlike a deep fryer, you don't need to use a lot of oil in an air fryer. Instead, the crispy and golden finish of your food is achieved through the circulation of hot air around the mesh basket inside the air fryer.

Most deep fryers require you to heat the oil up to a certain temperature before it begins to cook your ingredients. However, with an air fryer, you can pop the ingredients straight into the machine and the cooking will start immediately. So, you can save time and still get a delicious dish by the end of the process.

If you want your food to be extra crispy, you can add a light coat of oil around the food before you put it into the air fryer.

How Do You Use An Air Fryer?

Every air fryer comes with a detailed instruction manual that will tell you about all of the different settings that the air fryer has and the function of each button. You can keep the instruction manual close when you are using the air fryer to refer to when you're cooking if you're unsure how to operate the machine properly.

Although every air fryer is unique and will have different settings based on the manufacturer and the model of your machine. However, we've detailed a general set of guidelines that will apply to pretty much every air fryer.

1. Gather your ingredients and follow your recipe book up until the point where it tells you to place the ingredients in your air fryer.

2. Before you start making your recipe, like the mesh basket of the air fryer with baking sheets.

3. When you reach this stage in your recipe, put your ingredients in the lined mesh basket. Be careful not to overfill the basket, as this might affect the way the food cooks and reduce the crispiness of your dish.

4. If you're cooking meat or vegetables and you want them to be extra crispy, add a small coating of oil to the ingredients before placing them in the air fryer.

5. Close the lid of the air fryer and choose your setting and temperature. Most air fryers have pre-set times and temperatures that you can choose from to get the perfect crispiness of your dish. Most machines offer cooking times between 5 to 30 minutes and temperature settings between 180 and 250 degrees Celsius.

6. Allow the air fryer to do its thing. You can now relax and wait for your ingredients to cook. When your food is ready, you can enjoy your delicious dish.

Where Can You Buy an Air Fryer?

There are plenty of options when it comes to choosing an air fryer. Just a quick look online and you will see a range of machines from all sorts of manufacturers. Knowing which one is the best for you can be difficult. But make sure to read through the reviews on each product and check the specifications to determine whether or not it meets your needs and expectations.

Depending on the manufacturer and model, an air fryer machine might have different features and settings, so you will need to take a closer look at each option before you make a decision. Of course, you will also need to consider your budget and how much you want to spend on your new air fryer.

Here are some of the most well-known and well-loved air fryers:

- Philips Avance Turbo-Star Air Fryer
- NINJA Foodi MAX 14-in-1 SmartLid Air Fryer
- COSORI Air Fryer Air Fryer
- Black and Decker Purify Air Fryer
- Tower T17023 Air Fryer
- PowerXL Vortex Air Fryer

If you already own an air fryer that works perfectly, you don't need to throw it out and get a brand-new one!

What Are the Different Types of Air Fryers?

There are a few different types of air fryers that you can buy but there are four types of air fryers that are the most common. The type that is best for you depends on your preferred style of cooking and your budget.

Here are the main four kinds of air fryers.

Basket Air Fryers

Basket air fryers are the kind of air fryer that contains the mesh baskets that we have spoken about already in this book. They are by far the most common type of air fryer that you will come across and they heat your food using several heating elements and a large fan.

Convection Oven Air Fryers

The convection oven air fryers provide a combination of a convection oven and a fryer. You can use them for conventional oven baking or frying, and they are usually the kind of air fryer that is left out on the kitchen countertop because they look sleek and compact.

Paddle Air Fryers

Although less well-known, paddle air fryers are another great option when you want quick and stress-free cooing. They use a paddle that turns your food over to cook everything evenly. They're perfect for curries, stews, and chili dishes.

Oil-less Turkey Air Fryers

A unique type of air fryer is the oil-less turkey air fryer. As the name suggests, this type of air fryer tends to be used exclusively for cooking turkeys. It uses a similar cooking method to deep frying and leaves your turkey golden and crispy. Generally, they are suitable for outdoor use, making them perfect for a family BBQ.

What Can You Cook in an Air Fryer?

The options really are endless when it comes to cooking in an air fryer. You can cook everything from breakfast pancakes to lunchtime omelettes to fresh meat and veggies for dinner. You can also create lots of delicious, sweet treats for dessert using your air fryer machine.

When you take a look at all of the recipes in this book, you will see how vast the variety of meals and snacks that you can easily cook using an air fryer. Depending on what you want to cook, you might need to add more or less oil to the air fryer before you cook your food. Generally, meats require more oil to ensure they cook properly.

What Are the Best Foods to Use in the Air Fryer?

You can cook lots of different foods in the air fryer but there is a selection of ingredients that are perfect to use in your air fryer, such as:

- Chicken and turkey
- Fish
- Steak
- Bacon
- Eggs
- Tofu
- Stuffed pepper or stuffed aubergines
- Chips or potato wedges
- Bananas
- Doughnuts

Who is the Air Fryer For?

Air fryers are so easy to use that pretty much anybody can use them. Whether you're new to cooking and you're looking for a treat kitchen gadget to get you started or you're a pro chef looking for a new way to cook your staple dishes, the air fryer is ideal for you.

No matter how complex your recipes are, the air fryer will make things quick and simple. They're very easy to operate and are inexpensive.

Those of you who aren't very savvy with technology will still be able to navigate the easy settings on the air fryer. Even if you're not sure how to properly operate the machine at first, you'll get more comfortable using your air fryer the longer you use it. Before you know it, you'll be cooking delicious, crispy food without any stress.

Making Cooking Fun Again

The air fryer makes cooking fun again. If you're getting bored of throwing things straight into the oven or frying them in a pan, your handy air fryer will reignite your love and passion for cooking.

The air fryer gives you the opportunity to try out a wide variety of new dishes that you might never have tried before. Even if you've never properly cooked before and see yourself as anything but an inspiring chef, you will find the air fryer fun and easy to use.

Eating a Healthy Diet

If you love the crispy coating that you can get on your food when you use a deep fryer but you want to create something healthier, the air fryer is going to be perfect for you. Deep fried foods are high in calories and saturated fats. Whereas foods fried in the air fryer are much lower in both of these things!

When you use an air fryer, you need very little oil when you cook your foods in the machine. Most foods don't require any added oil at all to cook properly in the air fryer. If you want crispy meat or veggies, you might need to add a very small amount of oil, but that's all!

Therefore, the air fryer makes all of your dishes healthier and less oily, but just as crispy and delicious. If you've been trying to reduce your intake of saturated fat, or you want to lower your daily calorie intake, try switching out your usual deep fryer for an air fryer!

Keep reading for more advantages of the air fryer!

What Are the Pros of Using an Air Fryer?

Aside from enabling you to cook healthier meals, the air fryer has a range of amazing benefits. Here are some of these benefits.

You Don't Need to Preheat the Machine

Unlike when you're using a deep fryer that needs to be preheated before you can add any ingredients, you can pop your food straight into the air fryer without needing to wait. This is because you don't have to wait for the oil to heat up, so you can save time and energy when cooking your lunch or dinner.

You Can Save Time and Energy

The air fryer is perfect for those of you who lead a very busy life. If you're somebody who wants to reduce the time you spend in the kitchen cooking each day but you still want to enjoy fresh dishes, the air fryer is the most suitable option for you.

Because there is no preheating time required, you are also saving time by being able to throw your ingredients straight into the machine as soon as they are ready. Even if you are using a little bit of oil on your meat and vegetables, you won't need to wait very long for the oil to heat up before you can close the lid and start the cooking process.

The air fryer is much quicker at cooking your food than a standard convection oven because the mesh basket of the air fryer is much smaller. The inner component of the air fryer is smaller, meaning the hot air can circulate around your food more efficiently. The fan that is inside the machine also improves the flow of hot air around your food, helping to cook the ingredients more quickly.

Therefore, the hot air can circulate around your food more efficiently, giving you a cooked and crispy dish in no time. Whether you're cooking meat, fish, veg, or dessert, you can get an evenly cooked dish at the end.

The speedy cooking process creates a tasty, crispy coating on your dish, which is unlike any other kitchen cooking gadget. Before you know it, you will have a delicious, crispy dish, ready for you and your family to enjoy.

They Are Ideal For Any Diet

Because there is a wide variety of different foods that you can cook in the air fryer, it's the perfect piece of kitchen machinery for any diet. Whether you're following a vegan, vegetarian, keto, paleo, or low-fat diet, you can find lots of recipes to cook using this machine.

We've included a wide range of recipes in this book for all kinds of diets, but there are thousands more out there! You can cook a brand-new recipe every night for the next year with your air fryer, no matter what diet you follow. You will be able to create delicious food for every meal and snack using this cookbook and other recipes that you might find online.

If you're somebody who loves variety in all of your meals, you won't be disappointed with the wide array of different dishes that you can produce using an air fryer!

They Are Safe to Use

You don't need to worry about any oil spillages and splashes with the air fryer because the lid is closed shut during the cooking process. As long as you follow the instruction manual that has been provided by the manufacturer, you can avoid any accidents, burns, scalds, and fires.

They Are Easy to Clean

Most air fryers are self-cleaning, and all they need is a quick wipe down after use. As soon as your food is cooked and the machine has cooled down to a reasonable temperature, you simply need to wipe the outside and give the inner mesh basket a clean. The mesh basket is usually safe to use in a dishwasher too, so you don't even need to hand clean it!

They Are Compact

You might be worried about buying another gadget if you have very little space in your kitchen. However, air fryers are always very compact and can easily squeeze into a small space on your kitchen desktop or into a cupboard.

They're lightweight too, so you don't need to worry about breaking or damaging your cupboard shelving! They won't get in the way, and they won't make your kitchen look a mess.

What Are the Cons of Using an Air Fryer?

Although we are slightly biased and we will always recommend that you buy an air fryer and try out some new dishes, there are a couple of minor cons that we wanted to mention when it comes to using this kitchen gadget.

The two main cons of using an air fryer are:

- Potentially burning your food because you are unable to see the ingredients cooking when the lid is closed. This is especially risky when the ingredients are sitting very close to the heating elements inside the air fryer.
- Reduced healthy fat content in your dishes because there is little to no oil required.

Common Mistakes to Avoid When Using an Air Fryer

Here are some common mistakes to avoid when you're using an air fryer.

- Using too much oil (you need a maximum of one to two teaspoons of oil when using an air fryer)

- Cooking food that is too wet (the air fryer will not cause water to evaporate from your food)

- Putting too much food into the air fryer (this will cause parts of your food to be undercooked or will significantly extend the cooking time)

- Not cleaning the air fryer properly (you should clean the machine after every use, especially the mesh basket if you have a basket air fryer)

Recipes

Now you know everything that there is to know about air fryers, let's get into the recipes so you can get cooking as soon as possible!

Vegetarian and Vegan

Roasted Vegetable Pasta

Makes 4 servings
Preparation time – 10 minutes
Cooking time – 15 minutes
Nutritional values per serving – 387 kcals, 60 g carbs, 10 g protein, 15 g fat

Ingredients

♦ 400 g / 14 oz penne pasta

♦ 1 courgette, sliced

♦ 1 red pepper, deseeded and sliced

♦ 100 g / 3.5 oz mushroom, sliced

♦ 2 tbsp olive oil

♦ 1 tsp Italian seasoning

♦ 200 g cherry tomatoes, halved

♦ 2 tbsp fresh basil, chopped

♦ ½ tsp black pepper

Method

1. Cook the pasta according to the packet instructions.
2. Preheat the air fryer to 190 °C / 370 °F and line the air fryer with parchment paper or grease it with olive oil.
3. In a bowl, place the courgette, pepper, and mushroom, and toss in 2 tbsp olive oil
4. Place the vegetables in the air fryer and cook for 15 minutes.
5. Once the vegetables have softened, mix with the penne pasta, chopped cherry tomatoes, and fresh basil.
6. Serve while hot with a sprinkle of black pepper in each dish.

Spinach and Egg Air Fryer Breakfast Muffins

Makes 4 servings
Preparation time – 10 minutes
Cooking time – 10 minutes
Nutritional values per serving – 181 kcals, 12 g carbs, 9 g protein, 9 g fat

Ingredients

- 8 eggs

- 100 g / 3.5 oz fresh spinach

- 50 g / 1.8 oz cheddar cheese, grated

- ½ onion, finely sliced

- 1 tsp black pepper

Method

1. Preheat your air fryer to 200 °C / 400 °F and line an 8-pan muffin tray with parchment paper or grease with olive oil.

2. Gently press the spinach leaves into the bottom of each prepared muffin cup.

3. Sprinkle the finely sliced onion on top of the spinach.

4. Crack 2 eggs into each cup on top of the spinach and add some of the grated cheddar cheese on top of the eggs. Top with a light sprinkle of black pepper.

5. Carefully place the muffins into the air fryer basket and shut the lid. Bake for 10 minutes until the eggs are set and the muffins are hot throughout.

6. Serve the muffins while still hot for breakfast.

Vegan Meatballs

Makes 4 servings
Preparation time – 15 minutes
Cooking time – 15 minutes
Nutritional values per serving – 312 kcals, 30 g carbs, 17 g protein, 18 g fat

Ingredients

♦ 2 tbsp olive oil

♦ 2 tbsp soy sauce

♦ 1 onion, finely sliced

♦ 1 large carrot, peeled and grated

♦ 1 x 400 g / 14 oz can chickpeas, drained and rinsed

♦ 50 g / 1.8 oz plain flour

♦ 50 g / 1.8 oz rolled oats

♦ 2 tbsp roasted cashews, chopped

♦ 1 tsp garlic powder

♦ ½ tsp cumin

Method

1. Preheat the air fryer to 175 °C / 350 °F and line the air fryer with parchment paper or grease it with olive oil.

2. In a large mixing bowl, combine the olive oil and soy sauce. Add the onion slices and grated carrot and toss to coat in the sauce.

3. Place the vegetables in the air fryer and cook for 5 minutes until slightly soft.

4. Meanwhile, place the chickpeas, plain flour, rolled oats, and roasted cashews in a blender, and mix until well combined.

5. Remove the mixture from the blender and stir in the garlic powder and cumin. Add the onions and carrots to the bowl and mix well.

6. Scoop the mixture into small meatballs and place them into the air fryer. Increase the temperature on the machine up to 190 °C / 370 °F and cook the meatballs for 10-12 minutes until golden and crispy.

Spring Ratatouille

Makes 2 servings
Preparation time – 15 minutes
Cooking time – 15 minutes
Nutritional values per serving – 161 kcals, 20 g carbs, 5 g protein, 8 g fat

Ingredients

♦ 1 tbsp olive oil

♦ 4 Roma tomatoes, sliced

♦ 2 cloves garlic, minced

♦ 1 courgette, cut into chunks

♦ 1 red pepper and 1 yellow pepper, cut into chunks

♦ 2 tbsp mixed herbs

♦ 1 tbsp vinegar

Method

1. Preheat the air fryer to 190 °C / 370 °F and line the air fryer with parchment paper or grease it with olive oil.

2. Place all of the ingredients into a large mixing bowl and mix until fully combined.

3. Transfer the vegetables into the lined air fryer basket, close the lid, and cook for 15 minutes until the vegetables have softened.

Sticky Tofu With Cauliflower Rice

Makes 4 servings
Preparation time – 15 minutes
Cooking time – 20 minutes
Nutritional values per serving – 145 kcals, 18 g carbs, 10 g protein, 18 g fat

Ingredients

For the tofu:

♦ 1 x 180 g / 6 oz block firm tofu

♦ 2 tbsp soy sauce

♦ 1 onion, sliced

♦ 1 large carrot, peeled and thinly sliced

For the cauliflower:

♦ 200 g / 7 oz cauliflower florets

♦ 2 tbsp soy sauce

♦ 1 tbsp sesame oil

♦ 2 cloves garlic, minced

♦ 100 g / 3.5 oz broccoli, chopped into small florets

Method

1. Preheat the air fryer to 190 °C / 370 °F and line the air fryer with parchment paper or grease it with olive oil.
2. Crumble the tofu into a bowl and mix in the soy sauce, and the sliced onion and carrot.
3. Cook the tofu and vegetables in the air fryer for 10 minutes.
4. Meanwhile, place the cauliflower florets into a blender and pulse until it forms a rice-like consistency.
5. Place the cauliflower rice in a bowl and mix in the soy sauce, sesame oil, minced garlic cloves, and broccoli florets until well combined. Transfer to the air fryer and cook for 10 minutes until hot and crispy.

Chickpea and Sweetcorn Falafel

Makes 4 servings
Preparation time – 10 minutes
Cooking time – 15 minutes
Nutritional values per serving – 165 kcals, 10 g carbs, 9 g protein, 9 g fat

Ingredients

- ½ onion, sliced
- 2 cloves garlic, peeled and sliced
- 2 tbsp fresh parsley, chopped
- 2 tbsp fresh coriander, chopped
- 2 x 400 g / 14 oz chickpeas, drained and rinsed
- 1 tsp salt
- 1 tsp black pepper
- 1 tsp baking powder
- 1 tsp dried mixed herbs
- 1 tsp cumin
- 1 tsp chili powder
- 50 g / 1.8 oz sweetcorn, fresh or frozen

Method

1. Preheat the air fryer to 180 °C / 350 °F and line the bottom of the basket with parchment paper.

2. In a food processor, place the onion, garlic cloves, fresh parsley, and fresh coriander. Pulse the ingredients in 30-second intervals until they form a smooth mixture. Scrape the mixture from the sides of the food processor in between each interval if necessary.

3. Mix in the chickpeas, salt, black pepper, baking powder, dried mixed herbs, cumin, and chili powder. Pulse the mixture until fully combined and smooth. Add more water if the mixture is looking a bit dry. The mixture should be dry but not crumbly.

4. Use a spoon to scoop out 2 tbsp of the chickpea mixture at a time and roll into small, even falafels.

5. Transfer the falafels into the prepared air fryer basket and cook for 12-15 minutes.

6. Serve the falafels either hot or cold as a side dish to your main meal or as part of a large salad.

Air Fryer Cheese Sandwich

Makes 2 servings
Preparation time – 10 minutes
Cooking time – 10 minutes
Nutritional values per serving – 234 kcals, 21 g carbs, 7 g protein, 8 g fat

Ingredients

- 4 slices white or wholemeal bread
- 2 tbsp butter
- 50 g / 3.5 oz cheddar cheese, grated

Method

1. Preheat the air fryer to 180 °C / 350 °F and line the bottom of the basket with parchment paper.
2. Lay the slices of bread out on a clean surface and butter one side of each. Evenly sprinkle the cheese on two of the slices and cover with the final two slices.
3. Transfer the sandwiches to the air fryer, close the lid, and cook for 5 minutes until the bread is crispy and golden, and the cheese is melted.

Spinach and Feta Croissants

Makes 4 servings
Preparation time – 10 minutes
Cooking time – 10 minutes
Nutritional values per serving – 198 kcals, 17 g carbs, 6 g protein, 12 g fat

Ingredients

- ◆ 4 pre-made croissants
- ◆ 100 g / 7 oz feta cheese, crumbled
- ◆ 1 tsp dried chives
- ◆ 1 tsp garlic powder
- ◆ 50 g / 3.5 oz fresh spinach, chopped

Method

1. Preheat the air fryer to 180 °C / 350 °F. Remove the mesh basket from the air fryer machine and line with parchment paper.

2. Cut the croissants in half and lay each half out on the lined mesh basket.

3. In a bowl, combine the crumbled feta cheese, dried chives, garlic powder, and chopped spinach until they form a consistent mixture.

4. Spoon some of the mixture one half of the four croissants and cover with the second half of the croissants to seal in the filling.

5. Carefully slide the croissants in the mesh basket into the air fryer machine, close the lid, and cook for 10 minutes until the pastry is crispy and the feta cheese has melted.

Tomato and Herb Tofu

Makes 4 servings
Preparation time – 20 minutes
Cooking time – 10 minutes
Nutritional values per serving – 302 kcals, 7 g carbs, 12 g protein, 13 g fat

Ingredients

♦ 1 x 400 g / 14 oz block firm tofu

♦ 1 tbsp soy sauce

♦ 2 tbsp tomato paste

♦ 1 tsp dried oregano

♦ 1 tsp dried basil

♦ 1 tsp garlic powder

Method

1. Remove the tofu from the packaging and place on a sheet of kitchen roll. Place another sheet of kitchen roll on top of the tofu and place a plate on top of it.

2. Use something heavy to press the plate down on top of the tofu. Leave for 10 minutes to press the water out of the tofu.

3. Remove the paper towels from the tofu and chop them into even slices that are around 1/2 cm thick.

4. Preheat the air fryer to 180 °C / 350 °F. Remove the mesh basket from the air fryer machine and line with parchment paper.

5. Place the tofu slices on a lined baking sheet.

6. In a bowl, mix the soy sauce, tomato paste, dried oregano, dried basil, and garlic powder until fully combined.

7. Spread the mixture evenly over the tofu slices. Place the tofu slices on the baking sheet in the lined air fryer basket and cook for 10 minutes until the tofu is firm and crispy.

8. Serve the tofu slices with a side of rice or noodles and some hot vegetables.

EXCLUSIVE BONUS

40 Weight Loss Recipes

&

14 Days Meal Plan

Scan the QR-Code and receive
the FREE download:

Mary Stourbrook

Poultry and Fish

Air Fryer BBQ and Cheddar Chicken

Makes 4 servings
Preparation time – 15 minutes
Cooking time – 10 minutes
Nutritional values per serving – 314 kcals, 17 g carbs, 21 g protein, 13 g fat

Ingredients

♦ 4 slices white bread

♦ 4 x 100 g / 3.5 oz skinless, boneless chicken breast fillets

♦ 1 tsp salt

♦ 1 tsp black pepper

♦ 50 g / 1.8 oz cheddar cheese, grated

♦ 1 tsp garlic powder

♦ 1 tsp dried mixed herbs

♦ 100 g / 3.5 oz plain flour

♦ 2 eggs, beaten

♦ 4 tbsp smoky BBQ sauce

Method

1. Preheat your air fryer to 200 °C / 400 °F and line the bottom of the basket with parchment paper.

2. Cut the crusts off each slice of bread and place the bread into a food processor. Blend for 20 seconds or until the bread is fully broken up into crumbs. Transfer the breadcrumbs into a bowl and set aside.

3. Cut the chicken breast fillets in half and season with salt and pepper.

4. In a mixing bowl, mix the cheddar cheese, garlic powder, and mixed herbs until fully combined.

5. Spoon the cheese evenly onto the chicken breasts and fold the fillets over. Press the edges of the fillets down to seal in the cheese mixture.

6. In separate bowls, place the flour and beaten eggs.

7. Coat the chicken breasts first in the flour, then in the egg mixture, and finally, cover them in the homemade breadcrumbs. By the end, the chicken breasts should be fully coated in the breadcrumbs.

8. Transfer the coated chicken breasts into the prepared air fryer basket, close the lid, and cook the fillets for 10 minutes until crispy and golden.

9. Serve the chicken hot with a squirt of BBQ sauce on top.

Air Fryer Chicken Wings

Makes 4 servings
Preparation time – 10 minutes
Cooking time – 20 minutes
Nutritional values per serving – 213 kcals, 12 g carbs, 11 g protein, 10 g fat

Ingredients

♦ 400 g / 14 oz chicken wings

♦ 1 tsp black pepper

♦ 1 tsp garlic powder

♦ 4 tbsp hot sauce

♦ 2 tbsp soy sauce

♦ 4 tbsp olive oil

Method

1. Preheat the air fryer to 200 °C / 400 °F and line the bottom of the basket with parchment paper.
2. Season the wings with black pepper and garlic powder. Cook in the air fryer for 10-12 minutes until they turn slightly brown.
3. While the chicken wings are in the air fryer, whisk together the hot sauce, soy sauce, and olive oil in a bowl until fully combined into a smooth sauce.
4. Remove the chicken wings from the air fryer and coat them in the sauce.
5. Return the wings to the hot air fryer and cook for 5-7 minutes until hot and crispy.
6. Serve the wings hot with a side of salad or cooked veggies.

Southern Fried Crispy Air Fryer Chicken

Makes 4 servings
Preparation time – 15 minutes
Cooking time – 15 minutes
Nutritional values per serving – 344 kcals, 15 g carbs, 25 g protein, 15 g fat

Ingredients

♦ 200 g / 7 oz plain crackers

♦ 1 tsp fresh basil, finely chopped

♦ 1 tsp smoked paprika

♦ 1 tsp BBQ seasoning

♦ 1 tsp chili flakes

♦ 1 tsp black pepper

♦ 1 tsp salt

♦ 1 egg

♦ 400 g / 14 oz chicken thighs

Method

1. Preheat the air fryer to 180 °C / 350 °F and line the bottom of the basket with parchment paper.

2. Crush the crackers up in a mixing bowl until they resemble breadcrumbs.

3. Stir in the fresh basil, smoked paprika, BBQ seasoning, chili flakes, black pepper, and salt. Mix the ingredients until fully combined.

4. In a new bowl, whisk the egg well. Dip each of the chicken thighs into the egg to fully coat. Roll the coated chicken thighs around in the spicy cracker mixture until fully coated on all sides.

5. Place the chicken thighs into the lined air fryer basket and cook for 12-15 minutes until golden and crispy.

Air Fryer BBQ Chicken

Makes 4 servings
Preparation time – 10 minutes
Cooking time – 25 minutes
Nutritional values per serving – 334 kcals, 15 g carbs, 9 g protein, 20 g fat

Ingredients

♦ 1 tsp cumin

♦ 1 tsp smoked paprika

♦ 1 tsp BBQ seasoning

♦ 1 tsp garlic powder

♦ 1 tsp salt

♦ 1 tsp black pepper

♦ 4 x 100 g / 3.5 oz chicken breast fillets

♦ 8 tbsp BBQ sauce

Method

1. Preheat the air fryer to 200 °C / 400 °F and line the bottom of the basket with parchment paper.

2. Place the cumin, smoked paprika, BBQ seasoning, garlic powder, salt, and black pepper in a bowl until fully combined.

3. Coat the chicken in the spice mixture and place into the air fryer with the plain side down. Close the lid of the machine and cook for 20 minutes.

4. Remove the chicken breasts from the air fryer and brush the top of each fillet with BBQ sauce. Return to the air fryer basket and cook for a further 5 minutes until the sauce is hot.

5. Enjoy with a side of cooked vegetables.

Turkey Meatballs

Makes 4 servings
Preparation time – 10 minutes
Cooking time – 10 minutes
Nutritional values per serving – 299 kcals, 15 g carbs, 22 g protein, 11 g fat

Ingredients

♦ 400 g / 14 oz ground turkey

♦ 1 tsp cajun seasoning

♦ 1 tsp onion powder

♦ 1 tsp garlic powder

♦ 2 tbsp dried oregano

♦ ½ tsp salt

♦ ½ tsp black pepper

♦ 1 egg, beaten

♦ 1 tbsp soy sauce

Method

1. Preheat the air fryer to 200 °C / 400 °F and line the bottom of the basket with parchment paper.

2. In a large bowl, mix the ground turkey, cajun seasoning, onion powder, garlic powder, dried oregano, salt, and black pepper in a bowl until well combined.

3. Whisk in the beaten egg and soy sauce. Fold the mixture together until well combined.

4. Use a spoon to scoop the mixture into small meatballs and place them into the lined air fryer basket. Cook for 12-15 minutes until browned and crispy.

5. Serve while the meatballs are still hot with some spaghetti or in a large bread roll with some sauce.

Air Fryer Tuna and Sweetcorn Sandwiches

Makes 2 servings
Preparation time – 10 minutes
Cooking time – 5 minutes
Nutritional values per serving – 300 kcals, 23 g carbs, 10 g protein, 15 g fat

Ingredients

♦ 4 slices white or wholemeal bread

♦ 2 x 200 g / 7 oz canned tuna, drained

♦ 4 tbsp mayonnaise

♦ 200 g / 7 oz mozzarella cheese, grated

♦ 50 g / 1.8 oz sweetcorn

Method

1. Preheat the air fryer to 180 °C / 350 °F and line the air fryer mesh basket with parchment paper.
2. Lay the sandwich slices out on a clean surface.
3. In a mixing bowl, combine the tuna, mayonnaise, mozzarella cheese, and sweetcorn until a smooth mixture is formed.
4. Spread the tuna mayo mixture evenly across two slices of bread and top each one with a remaining slice of bread to form two sandwiches.
5. Place the sandwiches in the preheated air fryer and cook for 5 minutes, turning halfway through, until the bread is crispy, and the cheese has melted.

Crispy Salmon

Makes 2 servings
Preparation time – 10 minutes
Cooking time – 10 minutes
Nutritional values per serving – 112 kcals, 5 g carbs, 18 g protein, 17 g fat

Ingredients

♦ 2 x 100 g / 3.5 oz fillets salmon

♦ 1 tsp olive oil

♦ ½ tsp salt

♦ ½ tsp black pepper

♦ Juice 1 lemon

Method

1. Preheat the air fryer to 180 °C / 350 °F and line the air fryer mesh basket with parchment paper.

2. Rinse the salmon fillets and pat dry with paper towels.

3. Lightly coat the fillets on both sides with olive oil and top one side with salt, black pepper, and the juice of 1 lemon.

4. Place the salmon fillets in the air fryer with the seasoned side up. Close the lid and cook the salmon fillets for 10 minutes, turning halfway through.

Tuna Patties

Makes 2 servings
Preparation time – 40 minutes
Cooking time – 10 minutes
Nutritional values per serving – 247 kcals, 11 g carbs, 21 g protein, 8 g fat

Ingredients

♦ 200 g / 7 oz canned tuna

♦ 2 tbsp plain flour

♦ 2 eggs, beaten

♦ 100 ml milk (any kind)

♦ 1 onion, sliced

♦ 1 tsp chili powder

♦ 1 tsp black pepper

Method

1. In a large mixing bowl, mix all of the ingredients together until fully combined. Shape the mixture into circular patties.
2. Place the patties on a lined baking tray and leave in the fridge for 30 minutes.
3. Preheat the air fryer to 180 °C / 350 °F and line the air fryer mesh basket with parchment paper.
4. Transfer the patties into the air fryer and close the lid. Cook for 8-10 minutes until hot.

Sticky Soy Sauce and Ginger Glazed Cod

Makes 2 servings
Preparation time – 10 minutes
Cooking time – 5 minutes
Nutritional values per serving – 169 kcals, 4 g carbs, 20 g protein, 6 g fat

Ingredients

♦ 2 x 100 g / 3.5 oz cod fillets

♦ 1 tbsp olive oil

♦ 1 tbsp soy sauce

♦ 1 tsp dried ginger

♦ 1 tsp honey

♦ 1 tsp salt

♦ 1 tsp black pepper

Method

1. Preheat the air fryer to 180 °C / 350 °F and line the air fryer mesh basket with parchment paper.

2. Lay the cod fillets out on a clean surface.

3. In a bowl, place the olive oil, soy sauce, dried ginger, honey, salt, and black pepper in a bowl.

4. Coat the cod fillets in the spicy sauce and transfer to the lined air fryer basket. Cook for 8-10 minutes, turning halfway through.

5. Serve while the cod is still hot with a side salad.

Beef and Pork

Sausage Burritos

Makes 4 servings
Preparation time – 20 minutes
Cooking time – 20 minutes
Nutritional values per serving – 450 kcals, 31 g carbs, 10 g protein, 12 g fat

Ingredients

♦ 1 medium sweet potato

♦ 2 tbsp olive oil

♦ 1 tsp salt

♦ 1 tsp black pepper

♦ 8 sausages, uncooked

♦ 4 white flour tortillas

♦ 4 eggs, beaten

♦ 200 ml milk (any kind)

♦ 100 g / 3.5 oz cheddar
cheese, grated

Method

1. Preheat the air fryer to 200 °C / 400 °F and line the air fryer mesh basket with parchment paper.

2. Peel the sweet potato and cut it into small chunks.

3. Place the sweet potato chunks in a bowl and toss in 1 tbsp olive oil. Sprinkle salt and pepper over the top.

4. Transfer the sweet potato chunks into the air fryer and cook for 8-10 minutes until hot. Remove from the air fryer and set aside to drain on paper towels.

5. Heat 1 tbsp olive oil in a medium frying pan and cook the sausages for 5-7 minutes until slightly browned. Remove the sausages and set them aside on paper towels to drain.

6. In a bowl, whisk together the beaten eggs and milk, and pour into the hot frying pan. Cook the eggs and use a fork to scramble them as they cook in the pan.

7. Once the eggs are cooked, mix them with the potatoes, sausages, and cheddar cheese in a bowl.

8. Spread the mixture evenly across the 4 white flour tortillas and roll them each up into tight burritos. Use a toothpick to keep them together if necessary.

9. Place the burritos into the hot air fryer and cook for 6-8 minutes, turning them over halfway through.

10. Enjoy the burritos for breakfast or lunch.

Crispy Chili Sausages

Makes 4 servings
Preparation time – 10 minutes
Cooking time – 20 minutes
Nutritional values per serving – 245 kcals, 5 g carbs, 10 g protein, 13 g fat

Ingredients

♦ 8 sausages, uncooked

♦ 2 eggs

♦ ½ tsp salt

♦ ½ black pepper

♦ ½ tsp chili flakes

♦ ½ tsp paprika

Method

1. Preheat the air fryer to 180 °C / 350 °F and line the bottom of the basket with parchment paper.

2. Place the sausages in the air fryer and cook for 5 minutes until slightly browned, but not fully cooked. Remove from the air fryer and set aside.

3. While the sausages are cooking, whisk together the eggs, salt, black pepper, chili flakes, and paprika. Coat the sausages evenly in the egg and spice mixture.

4. Return the sausages to the air fryer and cook for a further 5 minutes until brown and crispy.

5. Eat the sausages while hot with a side of steamed vegetables or place them in a sandwich for lunch.

Beef Stroganoff

Makes 4 servings
Preparation time – 20 minutes
Cooking time – 20 minutes
Nutritional values per serving – 398 kcals, 17 g carbs, 31 g protein, 17 g fat

Ingredients

- 4 cubes / 800 ml beef stock cubes
- 4 tbsp olive oil
- 1 onion, chopped
- 200 g / 7 oz sour cream
- 200 g / 7 oz mushroom, finely sliced
- 500 g / 17.6 oz steak, chopped
- 4 x 100 g / 3.5 oz egg noodles, cooked

Method

1. Preheat the air fryer to 200 °C / 400 °F and line the bottom of the basket with parchment paper.
2. Boil 800 ml of water and use it to dissolve the 4 beef stock cubes.
3. In a heat-proof bowl, mix the olive oil, onion, sour cream, mushrooms, and beef stock until fully combined.
4. Coat all sides of the steak chunks in the mixture and set aside to marinate for 10 minutes.
5. Transfer the steak to the air fryer, close the lid, and cook for 10 minutes. Serve the steak hot with a serving of egg noodles.

Beef Satay

Makes 4 servings
Preparation time – 20 minutes
Cooking time – 10 minutes
Nutritional values per serving – 184 kcals, 5 g carbs, 17 g protein, 12 g fat

Ingredients

♦ 500 g / 17.6 oz beef, cubed

♦ 2 tbsp soy sauce

♦ 2 tbsp fish sauce

♦ 2 tbsp hot sauce

♦ 2 tbsp brown sugar

♦ 2 tsp garlic powder

♦ 2 tsp ground ginger

♦ 2 tsp ground cumin

♦ 50 g / 1.8 oz roasted
    peanuts, chopped

Method

1. Preheat the air fryer to 200 °C / 400 °F and line the bottom of the basket with parchment paper.

2. Place the beef cubes in a large bowl. In a separate bowl, mix the soy sauce, fish sauce, hot sauce, brown sugar, garlic powder, ground ginger, and ground cumin in a bowl until fully combined.

3. Coat the beef cubes in the sauce and spice mixture until all sides are covered. Cover the bowl with a clean tea towel or tin foil and allow to marinate for 10 minutes.

4. Transfer the beef chunks to the air fryer and cook for 10 minutes until browned and crispy.

5. Serve the beef satay topped with roasted peanuts and enjoy!

Homemade Crispy Pepperoni Pizza

Makes 4 servings
Preparation time – 15 minutes
Cooking time – 10 minutes
Nutritional values per serving – 213 kcals, 15 g carbs, 9 g protein, 8 g fat

Ingredients

For the pizza dough:

♦ 500 g / 17.6 oz plain flour

♦ 1 tsp salt

♦ 1 tsp dry non-fast-acting yeast

♦ 400 ml warm water

For the toppings:

♦ 100 g / 3.5 oz tomato sauce

♦ 100 g / 3.5 oz mozzarella cheese, grated

♦ 8 slices pepperoni

Method

1. To make the pizza dough, place the plain flour, salt, and dry yeast in a large mixing bowl. Pour in the warm water bit by bit until it forms a tacky dough.

2. Lightly dust a clean kitchen top surface with plain flour and roll the dough out until it is around ½ an inch thick.

3. Preheat your air fryer to 150 °C / 300 °F and line the bottom of the basket with parchment paper.

4. Spread the tomato sauce evenly across the dough and top with grated mozzarella cheese. Top with the pepperoni slices and carefully transfer the pizza into the lined air fryer basket.

5. Cook the pizza until the crust is golden and crispy, and the mozzarella cheese has melted.

6. Enjoy the pizza while still hot with a side salad and some potato wedges.

Pulled Pork, Bacon, and Cheese Sliders

Makes 2 servings
Preparation time – 20 minutes
Cooking time – 30 minutes
Nutritional values per serving – 245 kcals, 6 g carbs, 15 g protein, 9 g fat

Ingredients

♦ 2 x 50 g / 3.5 oz pork steaks

♦ 1 tsp salt

♦ 1 tsp black pepper

♦ 4 slices bacon strips,
   chopped into small pieces

♦ 1 tbsp soy sauce

♦ 1 tbsp BBQ sauce

♦ 100 g / 7 oz cheddar cheese,
   grated

♦ 2 bread buns

Method

1. Preheat the air fryer to 200 °C / 400 °F and line the bottom of the basket with parchment paper.

2. Place the pork steaks on a clean surface and season with salt and black pepper. Move the pork steak in the prepared air fryer basket and cook for 15 minutes.

3. Remove the steak from the air fryer and shred using two forks. Mix with the chopped bacon in a heatproof bowl and place the bowl in the air fryer. Cook for 10 minutes.

4. Remove the bowl from the air fryer and stir in the soy sauce and BBQ sauce. Return the bowl to the air fryer basket and continue cooking for a further 5 minutes.

5. Meanwhile, spread the cheese across one half of the bread buns. Top with the cooked pulled pork and an extra squirt of BBQ sauce.

Sweet and Sticky Ribs

Makes 2 servings
Preparation time – 10 minutes
Cooking time – 1 hour 15 minutes
Nutritional values per serving – 298 kcals, 5 g carbs, 23 g protein, 21 g fat

Ingredients

♦ 500 g / 17.6 oz pork ribs

♦ 2 cloves garlic, minced

♦ 2 tbsp soy sauce

♦ 2 tsp honey

♦ 1 tbsp cayenne pepper

♦ 1 tsp olive oil

♦ 2 tbsp BBQ sauce

♦ 1 tsp salt

♦ 1 tsp black pepper

Method

1. Place the pork ribs on a clean surface and cut them into smaller chunks if necessary.

2. In a small mixing bowl, combine the minced garlic, soy sauce, 1 tsp honey, cayenne pepper, olive oil, BBQ sauce, salt, and pepper. Rub the pork ribs into the sauce and spice the mixture until fully coated.

3. Place the coated ribs in the fridge for 1 hour. Meanwhile, preheat the air fryer to 180 °C / 350 °F and line the bottom of the basket with parchment paper.

4. After one hour, transfer the pork ribs into the prepared air fryer basket. Close the lid and cook for 15 minutes, using tongs to turn them halfway through.

5. Once cooked, remove the ribs from the air fryer and use a brush to top each rib with the remaining 1 tsp honey.

6. Return the ribs to the air fryer for a further 2-3 minutes to heat the honey glaze before serving.

Side Dishes

Crispy Cinnamon French Toast

Makes 2 servings
Preparation time – 10 minutes
Cooking time – 5 minutes
Nutritional values per serving – 231 kcals, 18 g carbs, 7 g protein, 10 g fat

Ingredients

♦ 4 slices white bread

♦ 4 eggs

♦ 200 ml milk (cow's milk, cashew milk, soy milk, or oat milk)

♦ 2 tbsp granulated sugar

♦ 1 tsp brown sugar

♦ 1 tsp vanilla extract

♦ ½ tsp ground cinnamon

Method

1. Preheat your air fryer to 150 °C / 300 °F and line the bottom of the basket with parchment paper.

2. Cut each of the bread slices into 2 even rectangles and set them aside.

3. In a mixing bowl, whisk together the 4 eggs, milk, granulated sugar, brown sugar, vanilla extract, and ground cinnamon.

4. Soak the bread pieces in the egg mixture until they are fully covered and soaked in the mixture.

5. Place the coated bread slices in the lined air fryer, close the lid, and cook for 4-5 minutes until the bread is crispy and golden.

6. Serve the French toast slices with whatever toppings you desire.

Air Fryer Eggy Bread

Makes 2 servings
Preparation time – 5 minutes
Cooking time – 5-7 minutes
Nutritional values per serving – 267 kcals, 24 g carbs, 15 g protein, 18 g fat

Ingredients

- 4 slices white bread
- 4 eggs, beaten
- 1 tsp black pepper
- 1 tsp dried chives

Method

1. Preheat your air fryer to 150 °C / 300 °F and line the bottom of the basket with parchment paper.
2. Whisk the eggs in a large mixing bowl and soak each slice of bread until fully coated.
3. Transfer the eggy bread to the preheated air fryer and cook for 5-7 minutes until the eggs are set and the bread is crispy.
4. Serve hot with a sprinkle of black pepper and chives on top.

Egg Fried Rice

Makes 2 servings
Preparation time – 5 minutes
Cooking time – 15 minutes
Nutritional values per serving – 198 kcals, 21 g carbs, 11 g protein, 7 g fat

Ingredients

- 400 g / 14 oz cooked white or brown rice
- 100 g / 3.5 oz fresh peas and sweetcorn
- 2 tbsp olive oil
- 2 eggs, scrambled

Method

1. Preheat the air fryer to 150 °C / 300 °F and line the bottom of the basket with parchment paper.
2. In a bowl, mix the cooked white or brown rice and the fresh peas and sweetcorn.
3. Pour in 2 tbsp olive oil and toss to coat evenly. Stir in the scrambled eggs.
4. Transfer the egg rice into the lined air fryer basket, close the lid, and cook for 15 minutes until the eggs are cooked and the rice is soft.
5. Serve as a side dish with some cooked meat or tofu.

Cauliflower with Hot Sauce and Blue Cheese Sauce

Makes 2 servings
Preparation time – 10 minutes
Cooking time – 15 minutes
Nutritional values per serving – 143 kcals, 9 g carbs, 2 g protein, 5 g fat

Ingredients

For the cauliflower:

- 1 cauliflower, broken into florets
- 4 tbsp hot sauce
- 2 tbsp olive oil
- 1 tsp garlic powder
- ½ tsp salt
- ½ tsp black pepper
- 1 tbsp plain flour
- 1 tbsp corn starch

For the blue cheese sauce:

- 50 g / 1.8 oz blue cheese, crumbled
- 2 tbsp sour cream
- 2 tbsp mayonnaise
- ½ tsp salt
- ½ tsp black pepper

Method

1. Preheat the air fryer to 180 °C / 350 °F and line the bottom of the basket with parchment paper.

2. In a bowl, combine the hot sauce, olive oil, garlic powder, salt, and black pepper until it forms a consistent mixture. Add the cauliflower to the bowl and coat in the sauce.

3. Stir in the plain flour and corn starch until well combined.

4. Transfer the cauliflower to the lined basket in the air fryer, close the lid, and cook for 12-15 minutes until the cauliflower has softened and is golden in colour.

5. Meanwhile, make the blue cheese sauce by combining all of the ingredients. When the cauliflower is ready, remove it from the air fryer and serve with the blue cheese sauce on the side.

Sweet Potato Wedges

Makes 4 servings
Preparation time – 10 minutes
Cooking time – 20 minutes
Nutritional values per serving – 112 kcals, 14 g carbs, 9 g protein, 5 g fat

Ingredients

♦ ½ tsp garlic powder

♦ ½ tsp cumin

♦ ½ tsp smoked paprika

♦ ½ tsp cayenne pepper

♦ ½ tsp salt

♦ ½ tsp black pepper

♦ 1 tsp dried chives

♦ 4 tbsp olive oil

♦ 3 large sweet potatoes, cut into wedges

Method

1. Preheat the air fryer to 180 °C / 350 °F and line the bottom of the basket with parchment paper.

2. In a bowl, mix the garlic powder, cumin, smoked paprika, cayenne pepper, salt, black pepper, and dried chives until combined.

3. Whisk in the olive oil and coat the sweet potato wedges in the spicy oil mixture.

4. Transfer the coated sweet potatoes to the air fryer and close the lid. Cook for 20 minutes until cooked and crispy. Serve hot as a side with your main meal.

Homemade Croquettes

Makes 4 servings
Preparation time – 15 minutes
Cooking time – 15 minutes
Nutritional values per serving – 306 kcals, 20 g carbs, 5 g protein, 7 g fat

Ingredients

♦ 400 g / 14 oz white rice, uncooked

♦ 1 onion, sliced

♦ 2 cloves garlic, finely sliced

♦ 2 eggs, beaten

♦ 50 g / 3.5 oz parmesan cheese, grated

♦ 1 tsp salt

♦ 1 tsp black pepper

♦ 50 g / 3.5 oz breadcrumbs

♦ 1 tsp dried oregano

Method

1. In a large mixing bowl, combine the white rice, onion slices, garlic cloves slices, one beaten egg, parmesan cheese, and a sprinkle of salt and pepper.

2. Whisk the second egg in a separate bowl and place the breadcrumbs into another bowl.

3. Shape the mixture into 12 even croquettes and roll evenly in the egg, followed by the breadcrumbs.

4. Preheat the air fryer to 190 °C / 375 °F and line the bottom of the basket with parchment paper.

5. Place the croquettes in the lined air fryer basket and cook for 15 minutes, turning halfway through, until crispy and golden. Enjoy while hot as a side to your main dish.

Sweet and Sticky Parsnips and Carrots

Makes 2 servings
Preparation time – 10 minutes
Cooking time – 15 minutes
Nutritional values per serving – 99 kcals, 9 g carbs, 3 g protein, 2 g fat

Ingredients

- 4 large carrots, peeled and chopped into long chunks
- 4 large parsnips, peeled and chopped into long chunks
- 1 tbsp olive oil
- 2 tbsp honey
- 1 tsp dried mixed herbs

Method

1. Preheat the air fryer to 150 °C / 300 °F and line the bottom of the basket with parchment paper.
2. Place the chopped carrots and parsnips in a large bowl and drizzle over the olive oil and honey. Sprinkle in some black pepper to taste and toss well to fully coat the vegetables.
3. Transfer the coated vegetables into the air fryer basket and shut the lid. Cook for 20 minutes until the carrots and parsnips and cooked and crispy.
4. Serve as a side with your dinner.

BBQ Beetroot Crisps

Makes 4 servings
Preparation time – 5 minutes
Cooking time – 5 minutes
Nutritional values per serving – 78 kcals, 11 g carbs, 5 g protein, 9 g fat

Ingredients

♦ 400 g / 14 oz beetroot, sliced

♦ 2 tbsp olive oil

♦ 1 tbsp BBQ seasoning

♦ ½ tsp black pepper

Method

1. Preheat the air fryer to 180 °C / 350 °F and line the bottom of the basket with parchment paper.

2. Place the beetroot slices in a large bowl. Add the olive oil, BBQ seasoning, and black pepper, and toss to coat the beetroot slices on both sides.

3. Place the beetroot slices in the air fryer and cook for 5 minutes until hot and crispy.

Cheesy Broccoli

Makes 4 servings
Preparation time – 10 minutes
Cooking time – 5 minutes
Nutritional values per serving – 99 kcals, 4 g carbs, 2 g protein, 4 g fat

Ingredients

- 1 large broccoli head, broken into florets
- 4 tbsp soft cheese
- 1 tsp black pepper
- 50 g / 3.5 oz cheddar cheese, grated

Method

1. Preheat the air fryer to 150 °C / 300 °F and line the mesh basket with parchment paper or grease it with olive oil.

2. Wash and drain the broccoli florets and place in a bowl and stir in the soft cheese and black pepper to fully coat all of the florets.

3. Transfer the broccoli to the air fryer basket and sprinkle the cheddar cheese on top. Close the lid and cook for 5-7 minutes until the broccoli has softened and the cheese has melted.

4. Serve as a side dish to your favourite meal.

Desserts

Chocolate and Berry Pop Tarts

Makes 8 servings
Preparation time – 15 minutes
Cooking time – 10 minutes
Nutritional values per serving – 255 kcals, 31 g carbs, 4 g protein, 15 g fat

Ingredients

For the filling:

- 50 g / 1.8 oz fresh raspberries
- 50 g / 1.8 oz fresh strawberries
- 100 g / 3.5 oz granulated sugar
- 1 tsp corn starch

For the pastry:

- 1 sheet puff pastry

For the frosting:

- 4 tbsp powdered sugar
- 2 tbsp maple syrup or honey
- Chocolate sprinkles

Method

1. Preheat the air fryer to 180 °C / 350 °F and line the mesh basket with parchment paper or grease it with olive oil.

2. Make the filling by combining the strawberries, raspberries, and granulated sugar in a saucepan. Place on medium heat until the mixture starts to boil. When it begins to boil, turn the temperature down to a low setting. Use a spoon to break up the berries and forms a smooth mixture.

3. Stir in the corn starch and let the mixture simmer for 1-2 minutes. Remove the saucepan from the heat and set aside to cool while you prepare the pastry.

4. Roll out the large sheet of puff pastry and cut it into 8 equal rectangles.

5. Spoon 2 tbsp of the cooled berry filling onto one side of each rectangle. Fold over the other side of each puff pastry rectangle to cover the filling. Press the sides down with a fork or using your fingers to seal the filling into the pastry.

6. Transfer the puff pastry rectangles into the lined air fryer basket. Cook for 10-12 minutes until the pastry is golden and crispy.

7. Meanwhile, make the frosting. Whisk together the powdered sugar, maple syrup or honey, and chocolate chips in a bowl until well combined.

8. Carefully spread a thin layer of frosting in the centre of each pop tart. Allow the frosting to set before serving.

White Chocolate Pudding

Makes 2 servings
Preparation time – 15 minutes
Cooking time – 15 minutes
Nutritional values per serving – 330 kcals, 31 g carbs, 12 g protein, 20 g fat

Ingredients

♦ 100 g / 3.5 oz white chocolate

♦ 50 g brown sugar

♦ 2 tbsp olive oil

♦ ½ tsp vanilla extract

♦ 4 egg whites, plus two egg yolks

Method

1. Preheat the air fryer to 180 °C / 350 °F and line the mesh basket with parchment paper or grease it with olive oil.

2. Place the white chocolate in a saucepan and place it over low heat until it melts, being careful not to let the chocolate burn.

3. Stir in the brown sugar, olive oil, and vanilla extract.

4. Whisk the egg whites and egg yolks in a bowl until well combined. Fold a third of the eggs into the white chocolate mixture and stir until it forms a smooth and consistent mixture. Repeat twice more with the other two-thirds of the eggs.

5. Pour the white chocolate pudding mixture evenly into two ramekins and place the ramekins in the lined air fryer basket. Cook for 15 minutes until the pudding is hot and set on top.

Milk and White Chocolate Chip Air Fryer Donuts with Frosting

Makes 4 servings
Preparation time – 1 hour 20 minutes
Cooking time – 10 minutes
Nutritional values per serving – 412 kcals, 44 g carbs, 11 g protein, 17 g fat

Ingredients

For the donuts:

- 200 ml milk (any kind)
- 50 g / 3.5 oz brown sugar
- 50 g / 3.5 oz granulated sugar
- 1 tbsp active dry yeast
- 2 tbsp olive oil
- 4 tbsp butter, melted
- 1 egg, beaten
- 1 tsp vanilla extract
- 400 g / 14 oz plain flour
- 4 tbsp cocoa powder
- 100 g / 3.5 oz milk chocolate chips

For the frosting:

- 5 tbsp powdered sugar
- 2 tbsp cocoa powder
- 100 ml heavy cream
- 50 g / 1.8 oz white chocolate chips, melted

Method

1. To make the donuts, whisk together the milk, brown and granulated sugars, and active dry yeast in a bowl. Set aside for a few minutes while the yeast starts to get foamy.

2. Stir the melted butter, beaten egg, and vanilla extract into the bowl. Mix well until all of the ingredients are combined.

3. Fold in the plain flour and cocoa powder until a smooth mixture forms.

4. Lightly flour a clean kitchen top surface and roll the dough out. Gently knead the dough for 2-3 minutes until it becomes soft and slightly tacky.

5. Transfer the dough into a large mixing bowl and cover it with a clean tea towel or some tinfoil. Leave the dough to rise for around one hour in a warm place.

6. Remove the tea towel or tinfoil from the bowl and roll it out on a floured surface once again. Use a rolling pin to roll the dough into a one-inch thick circle.

7. Use a round cookie cutter to create circular donuts and place each one into a lined air fryer basket.

8. Once all of the donuts have been placed into the air fryer, turn the machine onto 150 °C / 300 °F and close the lid.

9. Cook the donuts for 8-10 minutes until they are slightly golden and crispy on the outside.

10. While the donuts are cooking in the air fryer, make the frosting by combining the powdered sugar, cocoa powder, heavy cream, and melted white chocolate chips in a bowl. Mix well until a smooth, sticky mixture forms.

11. When the donuts are cooked, remove them from the air fryer and set aside to cool for 5-10 minutes. Once cooled, evenly spread some frosting on the top layer of each one. Place in the fridge to set for at least one hour.

12. Enjoy the donuts hot or cold.

Coffee, Chocolate Chip, and Banana Bread

Makes 8 servings
Preparation time – 10 minutes
Cooking time – 1 hour 10 minutes
Nutritional values per serving – 189 kcals, 17 g carbs, 10 g protein, 10 g fat

Ingredients

♦ 200 g / 7 oz plain flour

♦ 1 tsp baking powder

♦ 1 tsp ground cinnamon

♦ 1 tbsp ground coffee

♦ ½ tsp salt

♦ 2 ripe bananas, peeled

♦ 2 eggs, beaten

♦ 100 g / 3.5 oz granulated sugar

♦ 50 g / 3.5 oz brown sugar

♦ 100 g / 3.5 oz milk chocolate chips

♦ 4 tbsp milk

♦ 2 tbsp olive oil

♦ 1 tsp vanilla extract

Method

1. Preheat the air fryer to 150 °C / 300 °F and line a loaf tin with parchment paper.

2. In a large mixing bowl, combine the plain flour, baking powder, ground cinnamon, and salt.

3. Mash the ripe bananas in a separate bowl until there are no lumps. Whisk in the beaten eggs, followed by the granulated sugar, brown sugar, and milk chocolate chips until well combined.

4. Stir in the milk, olive oil, and vanilla extract before combining the dry and wet ingredients. Mix until combined into one smooth mixture.

5. Pour the batter into the prepared loaf tin and transfer into the air fryer basket. Cook for 30-40 minutes until the cake is set and golden on top. Insert a knife into the centre of the cake. It should come out dry when the cake is fully cooked.

6. Remove the loaf tin from the air fryer and set aside to cool on a drying rack. Once cooled, remove the cake from the loaf tin and cut into slices.

7. Enjoy the cake hot or cold.

White Chocolate and Raspberry Loaf

Makes 8 servings
Preparation time – 10 minutes
Cooking time – 1 hour 10 minutes
Nutritional values per serving – 189 kcals, 17 g carbs, 10 g protein, 10 g fat

Ingredients

♦ 400 g / 14 oz plain flour

♦ 2 tsp baking powder

♦ 1 tsp ground cinnamon

♦ ½ tsp salt

♦ 3 eggs, beaten

♦ 50 g / 3.5 oz granulated sugar

♦ 50 g / 3.5 oz brown sugar

♦ 100 g / 3.5 oz white chocolate chips

♦ 100 g / 3.5 oz fresh raspberries

♦ 1 tbsp cocoa powder

♦ 4 tbsp milk

♦ 1 tsp vanilla extract

Method

1. Preheat the air fryer to 150 °C / 300 °F and line a loaf tin with parchment paper.

2. Combine the plain flour, baking powder, ground cinnamon, and salt in a large mixing bowl.

3. Whisk eggs into the bowl, then stir in the granulated sugar and brown sugar. Mix well before folding in the white chocolate chips, fresh raspberries, cocoa powder, milk, and vanilla extract.

4. Stir the mixture until it is lump-free and transfer into a lined loaf tin. Place the loaf tin into the lined air fryer basket, close the lid, and cook for 30-40 minutes.

5. The cake should be golden and set by the end of the cooking process. Insert a knife into the centre of the cake. It should come out dry when the cake is fully cooked.

6. Remove the cake from the air fryer, still in the loaf tin. Set aside to cool on a drying rack for 20-30 minutes before cutting into slices and serving.

Chocolate-Glazed Banana Slices

Makes 2 servings
Preparation time – 10 minutes
Cooking time – 10 minutes
Nutritional values per serving – 200 kcals, 5 g carbs, 6 g protein, 8 g fat

Ingredients

♦ 2 bananas

♦ 1 tbsp honey

♦ 1 tbsp chocolate spread,
melted

♦ 2 tbsp milk chocolate chips

Method

1. Preheat the air fryer to 180 °C / 350 °F. Remove the mesh basket from the machine and line it with parchment paper.

2. Cut the two bananas into even slices and place them in the lined air fryer basket.

3. In a small bowl, mix the honey and melted chocolate spread. Use a brush to glaze the banana slices. Carefully press the milk chocolate chips into the banana slices enough so that they won't fall out when you transfer the bananas into the air fryer.

4. Carefully slide the mesh basket into the air fryer, close the lid, and cook for 10 minutes until the bananas are hot and the choc chips have melted.

5. Enjoy the banana slices on their own or with a side of ice cream.

Chocolate Souffle

Makes 2 servings
Preparation time – 10 minutes
Cooking time – 15 minutes
Nutritional values per serving – 401 kcals, 29 g carbs, 10 g protein, 13 g fat

Ingredients

♦ 2 eggs

♦ 4 tbsp brown sugar

♦ 1 tsp vanilla extract

♦ 4 tbsp butter, melted

♦ 4 tbsp milk chocolate chips

♦ 4 tbsp flour

Method

1. Preheat the air fryer to 180 °C / 350 °F. Remove the mesh basket from the machine and line it with parchment paper.

2. Separate the egg whites from the egg yolks and place them in two separate bowls.

3. Beat the yolks together with the brown sugar, vanilla extract, melted butter, milk chocolate chips, and flour in a bowl. It should form a smooth, consistent mixture.

4. Whisk the egg whites until they form stiff peaks. In batches, fold the egg whites into the chocolate mixture.

5. Divide the batter evenly between two souffle dishes and place them in the lined air fryer basket.

6. Cook the souffle dishes for 15 minutes until hot and set.

Apple and Cinnamon Puff Pastry Pies

Makes 8 servings
Preparation time – 15 minutes
Cooking time – 20 minutes
Nutritional values per serving – 301 kcals, 40 g carbs, 9 g protein, 13 g fat

Ingredients

♦ 4 tbsp butter

♦ 4 tbsp white sugar

♦ 2 tbsp brown sugar

♦ 1 tsp cinnamon

♦ 1 tsp nutmeg

♦ 1 tsp salt

♦ 4 apples, peeled and diced

♦ 2 large sheets puff pastry

♦ 1 egg

Method

1. Preheat the air fryer to 180 °C / 350 °F. Remove the mesh basket from the machine and line it with parchment paper.

2. In a bowl, whisk together the butter, white sugar, brown sugar, cinnamon, nutmeg, and salt.

3. Place the apples in a heatproof baking dish and coat them in the butter and sugar mixture. Transfer to the air fryer and cook for 10 minutes.

4. Meanwhile, roll out the pastry on a clean, floured surface. Cut the sheets into 8 equal parts.

5. Once the apples are hot and softened, evenly spread the mixture between the pastry sheets. Fold the sheets over to cover the apple and gently press the edges using a fork or your fingers to seal the mixture in.

6. Beat the egg in a bowl and use a brush to coat the top of each pastry sheet.

7. Carefully transfer the filled pastry sheets to the prepared air fryer basket, close the lid, and cook for 10 minutes until the pastry is golden and crispy.

EXCLUSIVE BONUS

40 Weight Loss Recipes

&

14 Days Meal Plan

Scan the QR-Code and receive
the FREE download:

Disclaimer

This book contains opinions and ideas of the author and is meant to teach the reader informative and helpful knowledge while due care should be taken by the user in the application of the information provided. The instructions and strategies are possibly not right for every reader and there is no guarantee that they work for everyone. Using this book and implementing the information/recipes therein contained is explicitly your own responsibility and risk. This work with all its contents, does not guarantee correctness, completion, quality or correctness of the provided information. Misinformation or misprints cannot be completely eliminated.

Printed in Great Britain
by Amazon

85421253R00064